The Text Beneath
Poems: 1992-2010

The Text Beneath
Poems: 1992-2010

Charlotte Barr

2010

Parson's Porch Books  Cleveland, Tennessee

Parson's Porch Books
121 Holly Trail Road, NW
Cleveland, Tennessee 37311

The Text Beneath—Poems: 1992-2010
© 2010 by Charlotte Barr. All rights reserved.
Published 2010.
Printed in the United States of America.
ISBN 978-0982-9413-5-5

No part of this book may be reproduced or transmitted in any form or by any means, electronic or mechanical, including photocopying, recording, or by information storage and retrieval system, without permission in writing from the publisher.

To order additional copies of this book, contact:

Parson's Porch Books
1-423-475-7308
www.parsonsporch.com

Cover design: Eric Killinger.
Photography credits: Cover photograph by Cheryl Barr. Author photograph by Loveless Photography, Murfreesboro, Tennessee.

To Mary C. and Mary W.

You do not know how much they mean to me, my friends,
And how, how rare and strange it is, to find
In a life composed so much, so much of odds and ends,
To find a friend who has these qualities,
Who has, and gives
Those qualities upon which friendship lives.

— T. S. Eliot

Contents

Absinthe, After Fifty Years	1
Arabian Days	2
Killing Flies in Cairo	3
In the Darkroom	4
Passages: In Memoriam MDB (1911-2002)	5
Monastic Dreams	6
Power Failure	7
Palimpsest	8
Chrysanthemums in Snow	9
Raining out to Sea	10
Infant with Ashes	11
Genesis	12
Details: In Memoriam RML	14
Late Valentine	16
Homeless Man with Dogs	17
April's Fools	19
Anhedonia	20
Seeking the Ancestors	21
Christ in the House of His Parents	22
To Number Our Days	24
Beauty's House	29
Baylor Gate	31
Career's End	33
Reign of Terrier	35

Gathering at Cowee Ridge	36
Tom Come Lately	37
The Crying of Wind	39
Saint Anthony's Day	40
La Toscana nell' Autunno	41
The Spacious Heart	43
Diocletian's Cabbages	45
Lightning Bugs	46
The Foxes at Forest Hills	47
A Grief for Pelicans	48
Blessing the Cells	50
In the Valley of Light	51

Acknowledgements

I want to thank Susan Collins, Dan Scott, David Tullock, and
    Eric Killinger for helping this book come to birth.

I will always be grateful to Jim Stover and the Baylor School
    for the privilege of being your poet-in-residence
    for fifteen years. I hope you will continue the tradition
    and find another writer-teacher to fill my shoes.

I am thankful to my two Marys, for always believing in my work,
    and for not letting me get away with weak titles for this book.

I am grateful to my friend, Victor Judge, for publishing two of
    these poems in Vanderbilt Divinity School's *The Spire*.

Absinthe, After Fifty Years

I met the Green Fairy once, when I was green:
In the Saint Georges Hotel, Beirut, that city so
Beautiful then, it was the Paris of the East.
I was fifteen, fecund with inchoate hopes and
Fragile fruits, before the bombs shook the
Cedars of Lebanon and life the boughs
Of my youth's verdant tree.
La Fée Verte is legal in this land again,
So I might stir its cloud and taste the sweetly
Bitter drink, and try if anise trickled on the
Tongue might unlock days and years in a
Proustian reverie: Of Beyrough sans
Blemish from our wars, of *la jeune filles*
Just then, about to bloom.

Arabian Days

Travellers, it is late. Life's sun is going to set. During these brief days that you have strength, be quick and spare no effort of your wings.

— Jalal-Uddin Rumi

Riding from Giza to Saqqara in those days, high sun, high spirits
And high strides were ours and would be always.
As the Step Pyramid had withstood Time, so would we outrun it,
Astride Kohl-ani, our swift, sand-stepping *Equus agillis*.
The Arabians' flaring nostrils and delicate muzzles led our
Desert flight from Cairo, from care, from custom and from night.
Hardy horses bore us; we rode high and hale in the ardor of our
Youth: O days so bright, Saharan caravan of chronic bliss!
As we approached, the limestone pyramid shone orange in the
Light and seemed a monument to life.
Yet hidden from our eyes were its funerary galleries
And halls of death.
Riding back to Giza, did we think at all of darkness,
Astride our bluish-black Arabians, their dark eyes set for home?
Did it seem then that life was anything but bundled light with
Worlds on worlds to roam?
It is fifty years since then; so swift was Time to catch us up,
That I'm baffled by his beating wings, so shaded by his breast
That I cannot imagine anymore the days I had of joy in full career.
As hooves in sand, our tracks will disappear.
However easterly we ride, our way lies west.

Killing Flies in Cairo

One afternoon, indignant at their ubiquity, fresh from clean America,
I swooped on flies that languished tauntingly around the balcony of
Our Zamalek pension: I crushed their smug faces with righteous cause:
These at least would not lay eggs in beggars children's eyes, or float
Undulant black clouds, over the mutton shanks in fetid butcher shops.
To my battlefield came peaceful Ahmed, our aged *sufragi*, unfurling
His knee-worn rug for orisons to Allah; he smiled at such exertion, said,
"La, Missy, there are always more pests than you can kill; it is the will of
God that we are plagued with them" (did he mean "and they with us"?).
I was sixteen and surprised by the fatalism of the Arab mind, distraught
At so much shrugging off of suffering, the expectation that so little can be
Done to make tomorrow different from today, that wars go on and on while
Am ha aritz, the people of the land, endure their leaders, tend their flocks,
Eat their beans, sip Turkish coffee, listen to their wailing music on ancient
Radios, eke a few piastres as they can, keep Ramadan, dream of Mecca and
Wait, Ins'Allah, for that Oasis which alone can quench the tongue of man.

In the Darkroom

Tilting the pan back and
Forth, back and forth,
I lift the image out of
Blankness as the paper rolls
Hypnotically beneath the
Waves, yielding to the acid's
Importunity.
I watch the portrait grow
And wonder what our faces
Would have been without the
Irritants, the rocking
Motion of the boat, the rub
Of caustic circumstance,
Astringency.

Passages: In Memoriam M.D.B. (1911–2002)

My father so long dead, and you so long in dying;
Yet so soon, too soon: my youth is fled with you.
Mother, wife, widow, friend, and, at the last, my child:
All mine to tend, fend for, do what tender things I could;
But by the end, I was no longer yours, not your only daughter,
But only one of those about the daily offices that duty does,
Or love: the voice familiar, the accustomed touch, a smile
Sometimes that pierced the fog and wrung a smile from you.
You forgot us one by one—your husband, sons, old friends,
And finally me—instead of us, your later loves, you went
Through all the dusty rooms of ninety years to find your kin:
Papa, mama, brothers, sisters, the ones who knew you first.
How could you have known you had survived them all? Now,
You know as you are known, the circle's joined, you're home.
Nature must have deemed hyperbole what my brother said,
"We're orphans in the storm"; for soft rains fell in Holy Week;
The day we buried you, the cloudburst came in blossoms.
The tempest was in us, bereft of you, who taught us how to
Name the flowers and the trees, how to hold in memory
Things fugitive as spring.
Our father so long dead, and you so long in dying;
How fleet, how final: our childhood leaves with you.

Monastic Dreams

My manumission is complete but for my dreams,
Which draw me back to corridors of silence, rows
Of veiled companions, the high, thin chant, meek
And folded hands, footfalls light in heavy clothes,
The comfort of constriction.
My waking world is wide, the broad way gleams
Wherein the heart's unhomed and, homeless, grows.
I rise to risk; athrill and trembling both, I seek
Commerce with the world, its joys, its woes,
The rub and spark of friction.
But often in the night phantasmagoric streams
Asperse me, as my shadow in procession goes
To burnished altars of the past; pale voices speak,
And soul, past reason's strength to interpose,
Implores their benediction.

Power Failure

I think of those Sarajevans in the winters of their
War, how it became unthinkable to read poetry,
Dance, or even pronounce such a word as beautiful:
Of the professor interviewed on the radio,
Who spoke in cadenced English like a dirge
Of having just felled the last tree in his garden,
One of the oldest trees in Bosnia; next he would
Start on the furniture, and after that, the books.
I stare at the transformer in our copse of trees,
As if my will could force the current through.
It is the twentieth hour of my heatless day, and I
Am hourly less smug about the scheme of things.
For me as well warmth could be all, fuel the coin
Of the realm, and art as useless as algebra;
I could be cold enough to feed the Fire God what's
To hand, turn Esau for a cup of boiling tea.

Palimpsest

The first time in Rome, one does the Catacombs.
I was sixteen then and too callow for old bones,
Too much in the sun to seek the subterranean.
The only grave I marked was the pagan child's,
Aged twelve, inscribed, "the green leaf forever."
The next time, after twenty years, in Trastavere,
I peered into an older Rome than young Cecilia
Knew, the city below patrician feet where seeped
The martyr's blood; by then I had some inkling
Of incremental martyrdoms and narrow rooms.
The third time I was forty and toured collegians
On their wide-eyed way around the Colosseum,
Along the *Via Appia*, and up the Spanish Steps.
Not down, not underground, for when you're
One and twenty, only what is visible is true.
I am thinking now I may outlive this anxious
And atomic age, but I do not think that I shall
Join millennial peregrinations to eternal Rome.
I will be where I am when the century turns,
Rubbing the surface to read the text beneath.

Chrysanthemums in Snow

On our hearing Puccini's threnody in concert,
My friend declared she knew now what
To send the mother of her son's best friend,
Who was lost in December in an avalanche.
May the flowers of the music fall like suns
Upon her frozen grief and warm the winds
That smite the South Arapaho peak, where
Rescuers looked two weeks before they said
They'd try again the spring to bring him down.
O searchers, say to those below: a young man,
Past the rigors of the climb, waits winter out
In clean repose.
Strings release, tremulously, as shaken petals,
The ternary notes; they melt as snowflakes do
Upon the cheek, becoming tears: *I Crisantemi.*
The Italian names all things as though all
Things were song; and music, that poorest art
For reason, speaks best for the stricken heart.
Puccini's loss became a melody; in his lament
We find a way to sing our tears; his elegy's
Our own: my friend so glad her own son lives
And for the sonless one so sad.

Raining Out To Sea

Like rain upon the open sea,
My tears pour out in vain;
Another love now fills your soul,
On mine you pour disdain.
My well of grief now overflows
With pain that you ignore;
The life we had forgotten now,
Those days will come no more.
When we were young you promised me
The dream would never die;
Your broken word is all that's left,
The last word's just goodbye.
Now all is said and done, you'll see
I'll mend in time, my dear.
I'm packing up my broken heart
And moving on from here.
But when the clouds pass overhead,
Though bright the sun may be,
I'll always think when I look up,
It's raining out to sea.

Infant with Ashes

Blow the trumpet in Zion; sanctify a fast;
Call a solemn assembly; gather the people.
Sanctify the congregation; assemble the elders;
Gather the children, even nursing infants.
                                            Joel 2:15-16

Midday, midweek in March, the eschatological moment:
Reminded that we are dust, and unto dust we shall return,
I receive my ashes, glad of one more chance for *metanoia*.
Sooty forehead bowed and soul-subdued, I find my pew,
Following a mother and her child returned to theirs.
From their inward gaze my eyes open on this pair: young
Women kneeling, infant asleep on the seat between us,
That same smudge blazoned on his brow as ours—the same!
But how? Is he a sinner too, so lately christened, callow,
Sweet? Whose zeal was this: the mother's or the priest's?
I come to this sight fresh from teaching Job, who saw
His virtue burned away and heard the Voice from the
Whirlwind call his purity illusion. Who is good? Do we
Call innocent those who are but ignorant of their guilt?
In Nineveh even the animals wore sackcloth, didn't they?
Grace to the mother who gathers her infant at the breast.
Lady of silences, calm in your distress that death sucks
Even the blooms of spring, I pray: *Ora pro nobis*
Peccatoribus, now in this noon of our new creation,
And at the hour when our hearts refuse to turn again.

Genesis

God is subtle, but he is not malicious.
— Albert Einstein

IN THE BEGINNING they were all beginners; no one was advanced.
Little by little they learned that Nature favors the firstborn, but
God prefers the second; so they had to learn deception.
Though the serpent was more subtle than any of the creatures
God had made, God had made him; he was Yahweh's protégé,
The world's first teacher, and Eve's first lesson after trees was
God's predilection for flocks over fruits and Abel over Cain,
Though not the reason why—or was it whim?
Sibling rivalry was couching at the door
And sprang.

AT FIRST the covenant was fragile, so the fathers built a fence for
Its survival; then as now, the last line of defense was dissimulation.
Abram had to say that Sarai was his sister, and they lived well in
Egypt so long as she was Pharaoh's wife.
As Abraham of the promise, he fancied the younger boy to Ishmael;
Sarah easily won the boon for Isaac, who in turn played his dad's
Old trick in Gerar: "Lest I die because of her."
His own Rebekah bested him, scheming to secure the blessing for
Her favorite son; who can fault her, for didn't the Lord ordain:
"The elder shall serve the younger"?

But who can forget Esau's exceedingly great and bitter cry:
"Bless me, even me also, O my father!" Didn't Isaac tremble
Then and see again, that blind old man, the shadow of the knife
Upraised so long ago and sorrow for Jacob who would follow him
Along the twisted way of Chosenness to the mad land of Moriah?
Lost to his mother, who called the curse upon herself, wily Jacob
Fled the springing beast to Paddan-aram; from Bethel of the dream
He woke and went to Haran, where he found his kinsmen at the
Well and loved at sight Rachel, the younger girl; the seven
Years he worked for her went swifter than a week.

But Uncle Laban was a schemer like his sister and had a ruse for
Putting Leah in her rightful place as first wife in his nephew's bed.
Even so, Jacob in his dotage forgot where favoritism led, and loved
Best of all his sons the dreamer, Joseph, who strutted in his pretty coat.
The envy of his brothers was the beast that drenched his robe in blood.
Yet the promise proved efficacious through doting fathers, meddling
Mothers, family strife and reconciliation; deception begat deception
Unto the fourth generation; the burden of the blessing was the root of
Jacob's limp, until Israel laid his right hand on the wrong grandson, then
Blessed them all and gathered up his feet into his bed.

At the end of the beginning the patriarchs and matriarchs must have
Known the truth of what the mystics say: "Nothing" is one of the
Names of God, and nothing ceases to exist at the moment of creation,
Meaning that creatures must then, for good or ill, make something
Of the world. Reading Genesis, one wonders whether it matters
To God that the Covenant came to fruition by so much mendacity,
So many wiles, and whether without guile the saving story could unfold,
Much less have been retold.
Is subtlety but the veil that hides the face of Him
Who was and is and is to come?

Details: In Memoriam RML

The universe is not rough-hewn, but perfect in its details.
                                     — Henry David Thoreau

Word of his death found me in Durango, and more than the
Pain of loss was absence, his and mine, from custom's ways;
Neither of us at home in our eastern mountains: I in this old
Western town, he gone to the uttermost West, past the river,
Valley desert, sea, and stars, to that undiscovered country.
It was summer, but the Owl (so the legend says) who calls our
Name can claw across the sultry face of mid-July, or any
Season he might please, the chilly summons: Arise, O sleeper!
Weary heart, bestir yourself; O seeker, turn to hear and heed
Such words as every wise man studies long to understand.
And he was wise, my friend, of all the friends and lovers I recall.
He was skilled in musical complexities; taking simple chords,
I'm told (he never played for me) he'd pluck out richer harmonies.
Books: so deeply read was he that all the world became a web of
Words and each new text the best he'd ever read, until the next.
Wife and daughter, son and grandson, he husbanded with care
And doted on—this careful husbandman—with a spendthrift's
Careless grace. His garden too he tended earnestly for Beauty's
Sake, his students nurtured he for Truth's; year follows year,
And then one day our husband, father, teacher, friend is gone.

Thinking back on him, one thinks of a book he loved and taught,
A line he must have savored as he read: "How life is strange and
Changeful . . . and the meaning of moments passes like the breeze
That scarcely ruffles the leaf of the willow." Life goes as life will;
Memory remains; affection's never lost; hail to you, dear friend,
Farewell.

Late Valentine

Long after you are dead, this valentine:
From one who dowered you in mute despair
With girlhood's store of unrequited care,
And read in sharpest pain love's surest sign.
Now time has let me taste both fruit and rind,
I long to tell you how the living fare;
Although diminished, dulled from lack of wear,
The cup we sipped in youth yet holds some wine.
You are unchanged, my love; I age, I age;
Yet I grow young when thought returns to you.
And here's preserved, like figures on an urn,
My morning love, your boyish face, on page
Where ink displaces juice of life, and new
Recounts old truths the heart once bled to learn.

Homeless Man With Dogs

I pound the steering wheel and say,
Man, take those dogs to a shelter, why
Should they be partners to your misery?
Long after they diminish in the mirror,
Disappearing in my backward look, the
Sight stays with me of the wanderer,
Bearded, crusted, bundle-bowed, his
Two dogs on a single lead, heads bowed,
Chained by brute devotion and man's need.
For days my mind devolves upon this
Love-bound trinity: will any pity them,
Or pass by as I did on the other side?
Now I sympathize, now disapprove, and
Daily watch for them, driving to my snug
House, where my two dogs wait to be fed.
Until one day I don't get home on time:
The unexpected car repair, dependency
On others, unsettle my complacency.
The old spectre of woman on her own
Returns: I could be, should circumstance
Conspire, a bag lady with a shopping cart.
Yes, I would want my dogs with me, don't
We all deserve a little joy? I see now why
The poor buy cigarettes, not bread alone.

A little glow against the night, pleasures
That delay a day no different than the rest.
My man,
Wherever you are hold up when that
Evening sun goes down, hold your dogs,
And run your fingers through their
Matted fur, and sleep, you three, upon
One narrow mat, be blessed in company,
On your own but not for that alone.

April's Fools

Last night, the first fireflies,
I thought they were stars,
Not expecting them so soon.
We captured them in jars
Summer nights ago, before
We knew how keeping mars.
Art and memory alone let
Nature stay.

Anhedonia

At dawn I search for what's left of the moon,
And flinch from the light of the borning sun.
I'm done with day before day reaches noon;
In a world of pairs I form a universe of one.
Funny that Faith should promise eternal rest,
When deeper requiescence is Despair's allure.
Hope would reside that can only be a guest;
Against her blandishment, my Heart, inure.

Seeking the Ancestors

Those who live there now are strangers to us,
Spending themselves to restore our homeplace,
Investing resources of their own to make what
Was become what is: walls enclosing them, a
Shrine for other sires, while not despising ours.
We visit there, we tell them what we know:
Where the butler's pantry was, which door then
Opened on the porch, how the dining room lay.
My mother knows these things, not I; she alone
Survives of all that generation and knows these
Things, and more, oh so much more than I.
She came there as a bride, approved by the
Paternal aunts, the parents having died, and
Welcomed by her husband's brothers, enlisted
By their wives as ally in the skirmishes of love.
Only she and one other gave them children, first
Our elder cousins, then my brothers, lastly me.
Two small broods, three boys, two girls besides
The one who died in infancy; a family's fragile
Linkage with its future, pentangled star flung
Out into the firmament of shining dreams.

Christ in the House of His Parents

In Millais' work the scene's so humdrum, understated,
The pain so muted, that only palm-readers or close
Readers of browlines get it. I do not mean to pun,
But I want to say it's offhanded, the terror thrown
Away. Seeing it first in detail, with two figures
And three sets of hands, I meant to write a poem
On hands. Yet this is not that poem, not *la mano*;
Not Wojtyla's landscape, that quarry being already
Mined by one for whom, now, the matter of split palms
Is more than academic. That poem is done, and the poem
Is a life, not mine. Others know what it means to say,
"Hands are a landscape.
When they split, the pain of their sores
Surges free as a stream."
One day in the sun, doing the daily round, the father's
Business, comes this intrusion on routine, this random
Hurt. The parents are surprised, as when in the old
Tales, the princess pricked her finger. The boy,
Perhaps, is not, his memory jarred to prophesies.
He just looks sad. His mother's forehead is a book
He seems to read, while his father sees to the cut
A slipped tool made. All she has thought is written
On her face. She is afraid for him.

Until today the bloodlettings were all a design,
One of their rites: circumcision or one of the endless
Slaughters of priestly sacrifice. Of Herod's rampage
They had been forewarned. But here was disorder in a
Home swept late and early that shavings not be left
To hide the scorpion.
Poems and paintings say,
In trivial moments more's concealed;
In manus tuas means not safety, but
By pain mortality is healed.

To Number Our Days

Commemorating the Baylor School, 1893-1993

*So teach us to number our days that
We may get a heart of wisdom.*
—Psalm 90

I

Learning is a liquid thing, flowing
As this river flows; below the clifted
School go barges, cradling wares that
Fuel the city's enterprise, while we
Indoors, year in, year out, enact the
Commerce of the mind. Oblivious to us
Who heave our big ideas from head to
Head, squirrels bounce from branch to
Branch, working their work too in tandem
With relentless play. They do not study us.
Within these walls we argue and surmise and
Think the woods are quiet; we might hear the
Chatter and the song if, breaking off our
Talk, we simply stood at campus edge and
Were obedient to the voices pulling us from
Pedantry to verge of elemental risk, where
Slippery verdure and the bluejay's cocky
Glance might temper our assurance that
Wisdom thrives alone in ratiocination.

II

Along the Tennessee the trees upend themselves,
Their tipmost branches brush the river's cheek;
When rain disturbs the mirror's face, they
Undulate like water snakes; storms past, the
Forest rests by dint of light and shadow in the
Stream; it is a trick the eye believes.
Cannot then we see, though many fathoms down,
The dreams that others dreamed before the rain
Of years came down on them? Will they who
Strove before us surface when we summon them,
And their endeavors shine in our remembrance?
Let them sing our history, for they are
Rio abajo rio, the river beneath the river.
O let these generations rise, their stories
Stir the song in us, of time and of the self's
Deep exploration; heed them when they say we
Are not here to seek but this day's wages, nor
Count our worth by what we comprehend.
This place, this land between the mountains,
Is not ours for conquest; our century is a
Blink of heaven's eye.

III

We build our towers, scribble words, and
Edify the young. And this is well, but
Listen: the water whispers news that our
Achievement rises not alone from our
Exertions, but from the graves of Cherokee
And Creek and Chickasaw, from energy
Of steamboat's throttle and the hup-
Two-three of greybacked men and boys,
Surging up this hill with colors flying.
The river's mouth, which may have been
Near Chattanooga, is unknown; a paradox:
The Tennessee, which is strong
Enough to seek it, never finds the
Sea, but is circuitous and doubles
Back, repeats itself, and finally cedes
Its waters to another's course.
Its stable banks are cut from stone;
Between them all is flux; in unity,
Plurality. Spirit of the River,
Send your Heraclitean fire to singe
The edges of our intramural space.
Whatever peace may be in strife of
Opposites be ours, as the rolling
Years leave us for a little moment
Here, alluvial anthropoids, to
Swim the while, before we
Drown in grace.

IV

The river is the same but not the same.
While the school's as old as all the years
Accrued to it, yet it is new to me, to you,
Just born today, for us to say: Thus did
I here, in this my moment, this my year.
Though midway in my journey I have come
To where my sire and sibling came in youth,
My father's feats, my brother's, yes, and
Their defeats are different. Our purpose too:
I am here because I'm said to know what
May be taught; they were here to learn
What could be known. I can find their
Faces on the wall and annals read where
Their dear names are kept. I can do more:
Resurrect by fiat of my words these kin,
Those former days, to feel again, to make
You feel, the sweat line on the runner's
Lip, the press of tape across his chest,
The winning; define the heft, the silver's
Gleaming in the hand, the pride reflected
In the cup; open to your memory windows
On the quad where old banners flutter
And desk lamps light the burnished
Pages of the past. Listen with me and
We can ascertain the footfalls in the
Corridor of those we knew. And sweet
As love is such remembrance, but sad

As love it is to think we cannot step where
They did in the river. I say we can't
With rue, but this with equal certitude:
Future gazers from these cliffs will know the
Bedrock and river's flow, learn to number their
Days, and toast on anniversaries our names.

Beauty's House

*For the dedication of
The Roddy Performing Arts Center,
The Ireland Studio Arts Center,
and the Music Building
May 8, 1998*

In Memory of Bill Ashley

*Yet, O Lord, thou art our Father;
we are the clay, and thou art our potter;
we are all the work of thy hand.*
— Isaiah 64:8

Pressure from the potter's hand enlivens clay,
First the drinking cup and then the vase,
From cooking pot to figurine: *utile et dulce;* [1]
Molding a handle here, and there a face.
Who would dream of angels sleeps on stone;
Music of the spheres starts in the throat.
The spirit's house is built of skin and bone,
And God wears all creation like a coat.
Art's truth is what, just quiddity, not why.
For soul a wordless language will suffice.
More to her than sentence speaks the sigh;
Soul is led by Beauty's hand to paradise.
Let our advice to the players be to play:
In a black box the motley world compose;
Revel in trying on Art's manifold array;

---

1. *Utile et dulce*: useful and sweet (Horace).

See both flower and the action in "arose."
Let not what shines hide polishing from sight;
The votive that the Muse demands is sweat;
Lovely as a swan's repose is the crow in flight;
The cosmic dance owes practice barre a debt.
This is our Globe, its roof a vaulted firmament;
We make here *mundus humanus*,[2] adorn the cave,
Rehearse earth's songs of laughter and lament,
Paint the universe in colors blithe and grave.

The river is Art's fountainhead and her foil,
Mocking the ache for permanence with flow;
Though our monuments are laid on solid soil,
They only stand by what their makers know.

Mark that we know this: the river is our ground;
Hand's skills are taught in the studio of the heart;
It is enchantment weaves the artificer's crown;
We learn the lines; life gives inflection to the part.

---

2. *Mundus humanus*: a human world (Nicholas of Cusa).

Baylor Gate

Those flowers, that gate,
These misty parks and motors, lacerate
Simply by being over; you
Contract my heart by looking out of date.
— Phillip Larkin

It gave us our entrances and our exits:
A façade that beckoned passersby to take
The road it opened on; bricks of red that
Framed a grey face and a name gave way to
Wooded paths, halls of learning, prayer, and
Sleep, and farther on to playing fields, marshes,
And the steep descent to river's edge.
Now to be replaced, this was the gate to
Williams Island Ferry Road where, on the city's
Northern border, are hid in mountain's shadow
Many dreams; there learning dawned upon us;
Wisdom hovered overhead, delicate as the heron
Resting on the lake; but silliness overtook us too,
Like those geese that tire of hanging in the sky
And ply their gawking circuit on our lower fields.
Beyond the gate a few old oaks still hold their
Ground that grew up among the Cherokee—
A people vibrant then who now are archaeological
Remains; these aged trees are patient with the
Young, mingling year to year with saplings
Planted class by class when fall comes around.

Now the gate synonymous with a school is near
Its close; scene of so many greetings and goodbyes,
Scaled by senior classes to have their pictures taken
As they take their leave; landscaping will ensue and
Grass reclaim a piece of road; what was a portal will
Become an ornament, and so it goes.
A little north a new road opens for our comings
And our goings; day by day another avenue unfolds.
Perhaps our pity for the old might be assuaged by
Thinking thus: what once was functional declines
To form, to simply being, beautiful and useless,
Holding its place the while and leading nowhere,
Nothing purposeful to justify its taking space,
Just there: against the landscape of our lives,
These lives that are themselves—usefulness aside—
Excuse enough to be.

Career's End

Some friends and some who are not
Ask, what will you do with yourself?
I say to them or to myself that I will
Still read but not grade what others
Write; build a sunroom and sit in it;
Gather my animal pack around me,
And my grand-nephews when I may.

I shall learn Italian and use it when
I go abroad this autumn (imagine,
Traveling in the fall!); not only on
Occasion, I'll be a writer actually,
And set aside each morning in my
Horarium (a useful convent word) to
Probe and plumb and process words.

I'll ply my garden; remember on my
Prie-Dieu friends and kinfolk gone.
I'll grieve for Tom, the professorial
Economist, who wrote me poems at
The Carolina shore after we stood
Where my parents met and danced
And fell in love on Wrightsville Beach.

I'll take my walks, drop in on neighbors,
And never never meet with those who
Have agendas (official ones, at least); no
Committees will I join or laudable causes
Publicly support (privately I wish all well).
I plan to read mainly books unread in halls
Of academe, swallow slowly, savor them.

I'm sure I'll still have anxious dreams of
Missing class or being unprepared (the
Counterpart of convent dreams in which
I'm missing habit parts, lose the place or
Drop the pitch chanting versicles at Lauds).
Waking, I'll recall diaphanous discussions
And dear auld teacher friends of forty years.

Fond students I'll be fonder of as the
Particulars of our acquaintance fade.
And by blessed forgetfulness the lazy,
Bland or baleful ones, those frozen in
Pubescence in my mind's eye, will seem
In my dotage as fresh, as rich in thought,
As promising as all of life did in my callow
Youth, when one September day in my
Twentieth year, I welcomed my first class.

Reign of Terrier

A pantheon of Scotties patrols the Rainbow Bridge:
Minnie Hootnanny, the matriarch, my prototype of dog,
Her runt, given to a neighbor over our mutual protestations,
Angus, her son, returned because someone took reserve for
Animosity, Paddington, chosen when I could finally choose,
And Pooh Barr, who was allergic to everything but
Paddington and me: these are late but ever held in memory.
Now reigning over heart and home, these three:
Paddy II, the rescue still reticent and stranger-shy,
His sister, Lulu Bascottie, the halfbreed who mothers him
And Fergus Finbar, master of mayhem, bad to the bone.
Along the way the odd spaniel and hound: Freckles, our
Gun-shy Springer, and Claus, beloved doxie kinder.
Yet I'm a Scottie person, admiring of the Diehard will,
Cobby build, grizzled coat and steady gaze, enamoured of
My breed's stout heart, square stolid stance, and haughty
Attitude, as varminty as his hapless prey.
Long ago, he ran to ground my heart
And carried it away.

Gathering at Cowee Ridge

For the Merins

Past Highlands, we'd turn at Cowee Ridge and take the
Wagon Road to Cloud High, through mountain laurel
And rhododendron, usually in autumn, always in a
Season of reunion and delight, a gathering of the clan.
Once the house held four generations: mother, son,
Grandson, great granddaughter: death has taken one,
Three are left and two of those estranged: brief, blessed
Unity once held, now fled, is left to us on film.
Thanksgiving dinners, jigsaw puzzles, grandnephews
All about the place: mundane, miraculous things:
Hiking Whiteside, sprawling on the banks of Emerald
Lake, the women's forays into town on shopping sprees.
The house our in-laws kept some forty years is being
Sold—too far away, too burdensome (truth told, too
Sweet to hold); yet Cloud High's household gods
Surround us still, its hearth, though thoroughly swept,
Still warms.

Tom Come Lately

What did I know of love's austere and lonely offices?
                                — Robert Hayden

Love came late for us.
Time's chariot overtook romance
And left devotion—not too late for
Travel, talk, a meeting of the minds.
Between us hovered his late wife,
My late dear friend, our grief for
Her, our mutual comforting:
There was always that.
And wistfulness—for all
That might have been in
Decades spent apart—
Apartness that our little
Now could never span.
And vague desires,
Yes, there were those.
Parting came too soon,
The swift onset of his bright
Mind's descent to gloom.
What was left was caring
For my friend, taking him to
Doctors, holding hands through
Silences of fear.

Then death,
Its drama and banality alike,
Execution of the will, all
That spate of documents.
And now the space between:
I on my side, he unreachable
Except to memory and prayer.

The Crying of Wind

Yeats says there is enough evil in the crying of wind.
And that is true enough in the news today: tsunamis,
Cyclones, hurricanes, tornados, rains that descend
On sodden fields, turning rivers to rampant seas.
Or rains that don't come, only the dry harmattans
Stinging the eyes of tribes who starve and stare
Into the cloudless light of their ferocious suns:
Too many sufferers for news to mark or us to care.
Of theodicy philosophers and poets have had their say.
Evil and good, impotent gods, one who suffers even,
Involve the wise; the rest of us, intrigued in our way,
Beseech our silent God to say what he believes in.

Saint Anthony's Day

For SMB

We beg you . . . that the soul may safely flee to you on that last day of affliction and fire, when the silver rope will be broken.
— St. Anthony of Padua

Ecce quam bonum et quam jucúndum habitare fratres in unum.
— Psalm 132

June thirteenth, my erstwhile feast comes round again,
And the anniversary day of my perpetual vows.
I was twenty-three; in the certitude that youth allows,
I said, "for all my life," and sure I meant it then.
St. Anthony doesn't reproach me, stays my friend,
And some companions keep my memory.
Today I think of them and celebrate what has been,
How good and pleasant still that story.

La Toscana nell' Autunno

For PJH

If one of us forgot the other would remind:
Do you recall the vineyards where we stood,
The villas glowing orange, those deep green
Exclamation marks, *cupressus sempervirens?*
Firenze, where as pilgrims we scoured San Marco
For vestiges of roots entwined with ours among
The ghosts of storied friars: Antoninus the holy
Prior and Jerome the mad reformer, Angelico,
Whose purest eye beheld the light and left it
For his brothers' eyes and ours as color, form
And grace: because of John our brother,
Remember Florence is all we need to say.
Before the campanile or camposanto, what first
We saw of Pisa was a Pisan with his flock of goats.
We won't forget the Piazza dei Miracoli, our mass
Together in Santa Caterina: such wonders flowed
For us from the Ligurian Sea, along the Arno,
And into the stream of memory: Siena where we
Gathered in the shell of Piazza del Campo and
Walked to the Duomo to pray; my disappointment
That the Palio is not run in autumn assuaged by
My birthday being the very date the horses race.

High San Gimignano we'll remember too, above
The Elsa Valley where the saffron grows.
We were pilgrims there, in Tuscany that fall,
On the journey marking my retirement from
The active life and presaging your sabbatical.
Ineluctably, we're changed, for at our core,
The memory is *semper virens*; green and tall,
Pietro and Carlotta will live forevermore.

The Spacious Heart

In Memory of Joe Gawrys

I am Joseph, your brother.
— Genesis 45:4

The road I take to paradise is bright with flowers.
— Sokin

This year you wanted to see the lotus on the other side.
And we, who wanted you to stay, had to let you go.
Swimmer, you are too far out to sea for us to know
Whether you have found another shore or a Guide,
Who beckons you go deeper now, not farther, below
The blossom, down, down to where the tendrils hide
That hold the lotus soul.
Seen another way, the incense of you life floats up
And up, past water, earth, on air your soul ascends.
Space being a construct that the intellect pretends
To know, we hold the mystery in a fragile cup.
We hold your memory that way, your friends
Remember you before death intervened, abrupt,
Although awaited.
Only you were ready, for you had studied death
And worn this world as a garment loosely made.
Having willed all creatures happy, having paid
The boatman, you were off; we, although bereft,
Stood outside our tears to hear what we had prayed:

" I am at peace," and finally the exchange of breath
For silence.

Diocletian's Cabbages

If you could show the cabbage I planted with my own hands to your emperor, he definitely wouldn't dare suggest I replace the peace and happiness of this place with the storms of a never-satisfied greed.
— Diocletian

In our retirement my friend and I visited the place of his, sailing the Dalmatian coast
To Split, where, not to be irreverent, one could say that Diocletian split the scene of
Power, pomp and persecution, put the Adriatic between himself and Rome, and
Planted cabbages; he called them *brassicas* and the land around them Salonae.
The modern name Croatia is less mellifluous but the place as sunny and serene as
When he came there, weary with empire, to seek his plebian past and peace.
Persecution proved a fruitless exercise; the Christians grew like weeds.
Here at least the soil responded to a farmer's will; here at last could
Diocles the soldier sheath his sword, having learned by wielding it
That water wrought a sweeter recompense than blood. Perhaps
He guessed as well that history laughs at no one more than Caesars.
The church of St. Dominus, his martyr, houses Diocletian's tomb.

Lightning Bugs

*I placed a jar in Tennessee
And round it was, upon a hill.
It made the slovenly wilderness
Surround that hill.*

— Wallace Stevens

That's what they were, lightning bugs, to us in Tennessee.
Yankees called them fireflies, not us, and we caught them in
Jars in Tennessee, wide-mouth jars, of a summer night so
We could watch their light and wish upon it like a private
Star if we were girls, and brag who had the most if we were
Boys, who didn't care if they died and made fun of the
Girls for worrying about them and letting them go and go
On glowing, our little stars, all the summer long.
Once in the Smokies we got to see them synchronize their
Glow, and that was a wonderment to behold, and no one
Wanted to hold them then but wanted them always free;
And that is how I see them now, in my backyard, now
I am back in Tennessee; with dimmer sight I yet can see
How many stars I could not reach and count the lives
I've lost who were, it seemed in childhood, as fixed as
Those mountains and not as evanescent as these bugs.

The Foxes at Forest Hills

I am visiting the dead on a cold March day,
When the sun is out, then in, and winds are
Shaking the dogwood blooms about.
Suddenly, three gray heads emerge among
The graves, followed out of the ground by
Bodies round, fuzz clad, and cautiously
Glad to be out of their cozy den and up
In the bracing air.
I go very still, unsure what breed of baby
This can be—not pup or kitten certainly—
Burrow bred: mole or gopher, badger,
Woodchuck? Puzzled by the undefined
Anatomy all mammal infants share,
I stare at these in ignorant wonderment
Until their mother, narrow nosed and
Blazing red, appears.
A vixen joins her kits, and I, a fan of
Foxes since a child, catch my breath
In joy to be so near the elusive, shy,
And secretive lady of the warrened
Woods, seen rarely in these parts.
I carry the vision with me to this
Day: the mother fox, her brood,
Life's insidious intrusion into
Death's domain.

A Grief for Pelicans

> *Like what tender tales tell of the Pelican?*
> *Bathe me, Jesus Lord, in what Thy Bosom ran?*
> *Blood that but one drop of has the pow'r to win?*
> *All the world forgiveness of its world of sin.*
> — St. Thomas Aquinas, *Adoro Te*
> (Gerard Manley Hopkins, trans.)

> *This Sea that bares her bosom to the moon,*
> *The winds that will be howling at all hours,*
> *And are up-gathered now like sleeping flowers,*
> *For this, for everything, we are out of tune;*
> — William Wordsworth

> *And all is seared with trade; bleared, smeared with toil;*
> *And wears man's smudge and shares man's smell; . . .*
> — G. M. Hopkins

And all is smeared with oil; this sea that gave us bounty
Without end is smudged with the effulgence of our greed.
These pelicans that balance on our wires now swoop to feed
At their own risk. Social birds, they follow one another to
Their doom in open waters and marshy reaches of the Gulf.

This gulf has ever wrapped our southern shores in warmth
And spilled her wares in traps, trawls and nets of shrimpers,
Oystermen, crabbers, and her fecund waters' fishermen:
Houma, Cajun, Greek, Yugoslavian and Vietnamese,
People of the bayous, breaks, beaches, and lagoons.
This was my gulf too, my playground, the Acadia of my
Youth: Anna Maria, where three children romped and

Two were nearly drowned in the undertow, where the
War waged elsewhere while we waded and watched our
Mother beachcomb and gather cockles for coquina stew.
My grief for this time gone abides, but greater still my
Grief for the pelican, who is the sprit of the place, who
In Christian iconography strikes her breast to feed
Her young, whose blood is balm and sacrament like
Our Savior's own: yes, this clumsy bird, who is only
Elegant in flight, is left to flap her ineffectual wings
In sludge, surely causing Christ himself to weep.

Blessing the Cells

In my dream I am blessing the cells as once I did
In another life: Saying, "Ave Maria" and signing
The cross on their curtains with the blessing of
Water in the profound silence of convent rest.
I send my sisters to sleep with these words, this
Shake of the wrist, this wish for their fretless
Sleep until dawn.
In the morning of this other life, I would rise
To ring the bell, calling them back to the
Waking life we all shared: to duty and day
And the daily round of communal prayer.
It was what it was: delight and despair and
Fondness and fear of not being all we had
Promised to be.
I am not what I promised to be in my
Floruit but believe I may come to the
Feast and be let in because of my
Friend, Whose love led me there
By a devious way, Who knows
My desire despite many turns to be
Blest and be staid.

In the Valley of Light

Brainerd 1945-1960

I am speaking not of Paul Bunyan's Brainerd but of ours,
In that childhood place beyond the Ridge after the War and
Before the time of turmoil, when we walked to school and
Played in Conner Field and boys sneaked off to the Quarry
To swim in the pit so deep they never found the bottom.
Our fathers worked in town at TVA or Provident or the
Dome Building, where the air was dirty, and then came
Home to clean streets and wives who cooked and children
Dressed for dinner.
Our corner of this sweet suburbia was Catholic mostly,
A veritable Vatican Valley with streets named Notre
Dame and Madonna Avenue. There was no singer by that
Name, not then, but only Perry Como and Eddie Fisher,
Bing Crosby and the crooners, who assured us that sunny
Days and starry nights made up the world; then Doo Wop
Overtook us with huge melodious tremulous songs of
Love; The Platters had the magic touch, transporting us
At twilight time.
Our new all-electric homes were stretched out from the
Hub, our church and school, Our Lady of Perpetual Help.
And she seemed always there to succor us; in May, we
Sang her hymns and brought her flowers of the rarest
From our mothers' gardens.

The nearby public school was our dreaded enemy:
Anna B. Lacey, named for a woman too, but merely
A mortal one. They called us the Old Lady's Poor
House, and we called them Anna Bum Lazy, all in
Good fun, or not.
In those days, our little world was only reached by
Passing through a tunnel under Missionary Ridge,
Into the region where the Cherokee children once
Had lived and learned. Exile and adulthood came
Too soon for them and us.

About the Author

Charlotte Barr was born August 16, 1942, in Knoxville, Tennessee. Soon after, her family moved to Chattanooga, where her father was employed by the Tennessee Valley Authority. As a small child, Charlotte spent several winters with her mother and brothers in Anna Maria, a barrier island off Florida's gulf coast. During high school, she lived for a year in Cairo, Egypt. She graduated from Notre Dame High School in Chattanooga in 1960.

From 1960 to 1990, Charlotte belonged to a religious order in Nashville, where she was known in religion as Sister Mary Anthony, OP. She earned her Bachelor of Arts in English at George Peabody College for Teachers, now Peabody at Vanderbilt. Charlotte holds an MA in English from the University of Memphis and an MA in Biblical Studies from Providence College in Rhode Island.

Charlotte was a teacher for over forty years, most notably at St. Cecelia Academy and Aquinas College on Nashville's Dominican Campus. After leaving St. Cecilia, Charlotte taught for two years at the Webb School in Bell Buckle, Tennessee. Since 1992, she has taught at the Baylor School in Chattanooga, where she held the position of poet-in-residence. Charlotte retired from teaching in 2007.

During her novitiate year, Charlotte began seriously to write poetry. Her early convent poems appeared in the collection, *Brief Blue Season*, in 1966. Over the years, Charlotte's work has been published in several periodicals and journals, including *The Sewanee Review*, *The Cumberland Review*, *The Distillery*, and *The Spire*, a publication of the Vanderbilt Divinity School. Two volumes of poetry, *Sister Woman* (1989), and *The Bell Buckle Years* (1992), were published by Maggi Vaughn at Iris Press.

www.ingramcontent.com/pod-product-compliance
Lightning Source LLC
Chambersburg PA
CBHW021026090426
42738CB00007B/917